New Orleans Remembered

by Eugénie R. Rocherolle

kjos Neil A. Kjos Music Company

About the Composer

Eugénie Ricau Rocherolle loves to write for the piano, although she has also enjoyed writing many published pieces for chorus and band. Her listening experiences as she was growing up in New Orleans—from recordings of the great masters that her family played to the prevalent New Orleans jazz—are evident in her colorful compositions.

Her home now is in Wilton, Connecticut, where she teaches piano. Prior to raising a family, Mrs. Rocherolle graduated from Newcomb College of Tulane University, with a year of study in Paris.

As she wrote *New Orleans Remembered*, Mrs. Rocherolle tried to capture the music of early 20th century New Orleans, starting with ragtime and including blues, spirituals, and a touch of nostalgia.

For other music by Eugénie Rocherolle, see the back cover.

In memory of my dear aunt "Veva," Marie Vivian Schlegel Carpenter, who so loved New Orleans

New Orleans Remembered

Contents

ISBN 0-8497-6167-0

Muddy River Blues

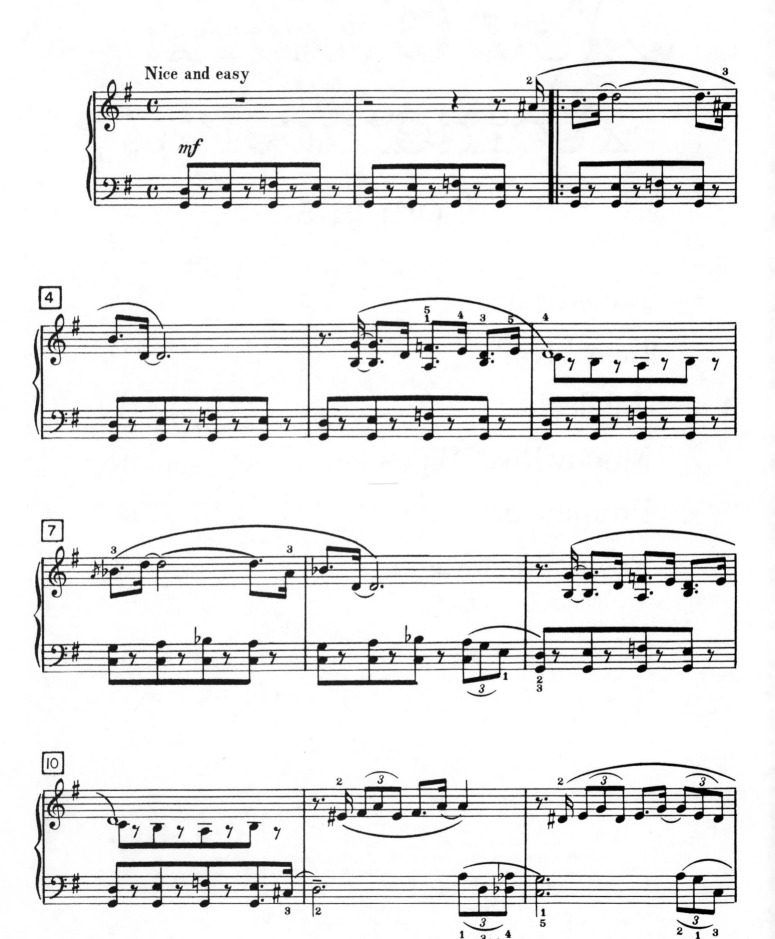

Promenade

Smoothly and with feeling

with pedal

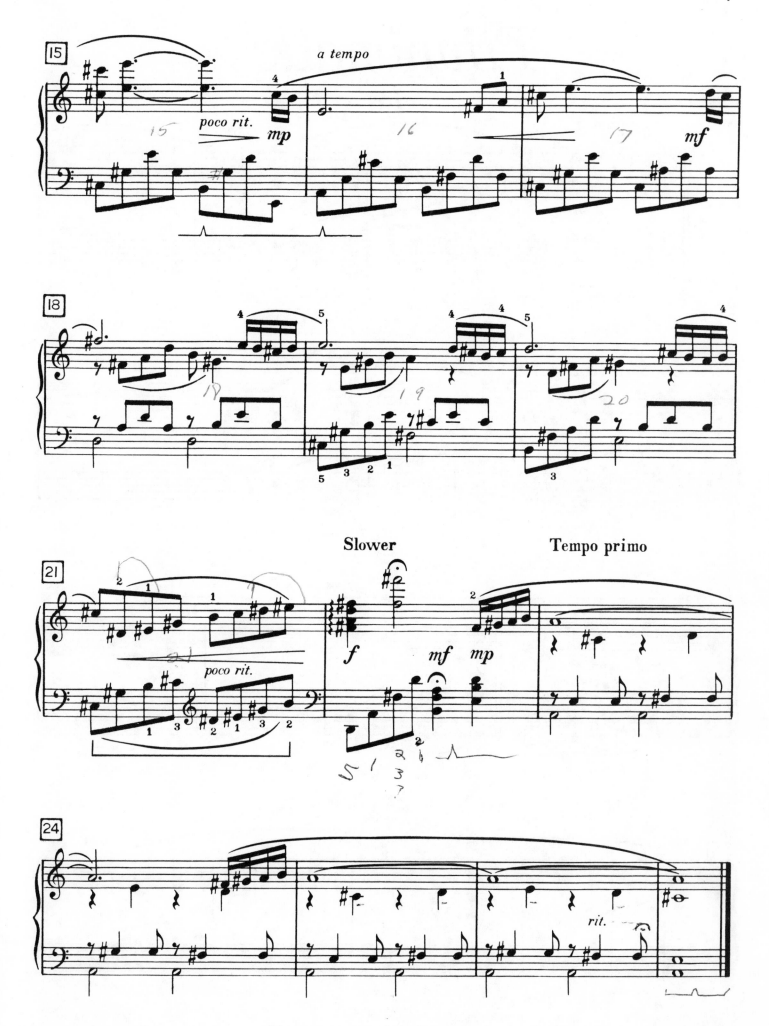

Jubilee!

Easy Livin'

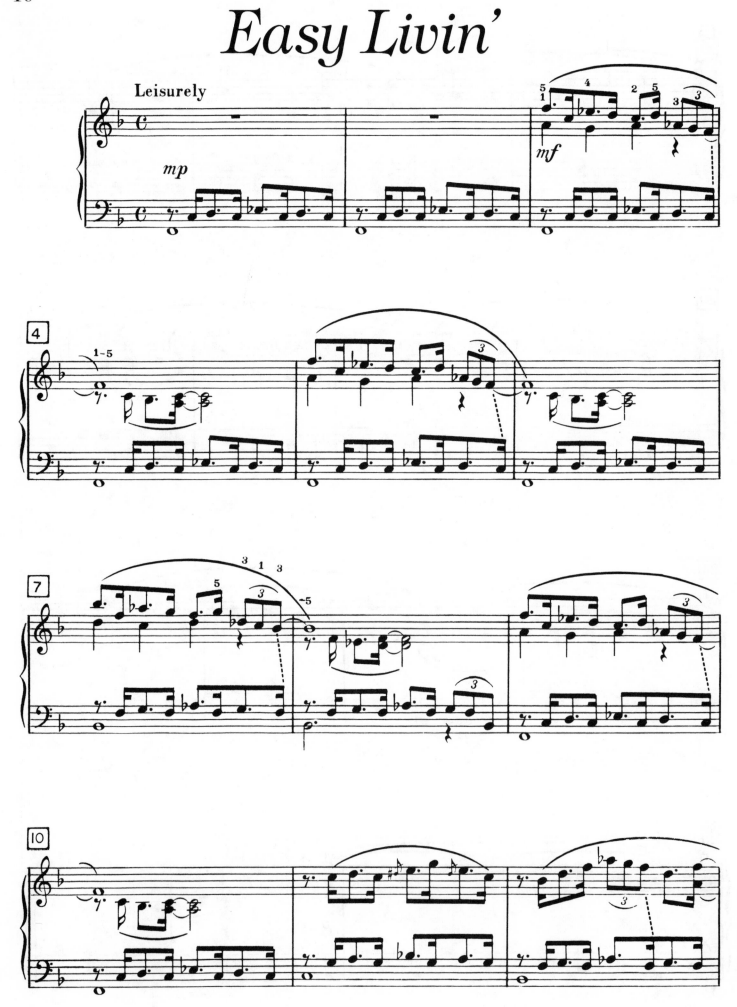

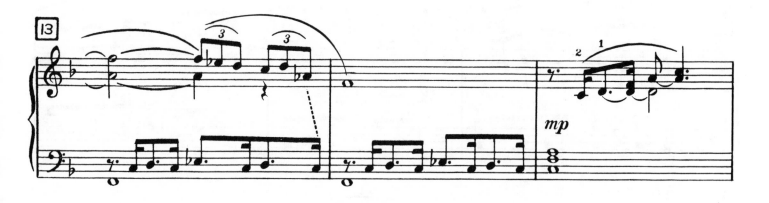

Royal Street Rag

Day's End